AN INCREDIBLY

ILLUMINATING BOOK OF

DREAMS

FOR THOSE
WHO BELIEVE
THAT ALL
SUBCONSCIOUS
THOUGHTS ARE
REALLY ABOUT SEX

Author: Kenton Bamford
Managing Editor: Simon Melhuish
Series Editor: Lee Linford
Design: Alan Shiner
Illustrations: Gary Sherwood
Additional contributor: Christine Pountney

Designed and compiled by
Mad Moose Press
for
Lagoon Books
PO Box 311, KT2 5QW, UK
PO Box 990676, Boston, MA 02199, USA

ISBN: 1-904139-27-2

www.madmoosepress.com
www.lagoongames.com

Printed in Hong Kong

AN INCREDIBLY

ILLUMINATING BOOK OF

DREAMS

FOR THOSE

WHO BELIEVE

THAT ALL

SUBCONSCIOUS

THOUGHTS ARE

REALLY ABOUT SEX

Somebody set fire to your socks while you were skinny dipping in a lake of raspberry flavoured chocolate. A kindly passer-by mistook your cries of "stop sock vandal" for "help, I'm drowning in confectionery heaven" and threw a cinnamon doughnut life saver to your rescue.

Unfortunately, his aim wasn't so good, the life saver knocked out your front teeth and sent you hurtling over the edge of a raging chocolate waterfall, falling hundreds of feet into a plunge pool surrounded by hungry bears and rampant camels.

Lady luck didn't desert you entirely, however, as you appeared to be invisible to the bears. The camels couldn't be fooled, but were far more interested in your doughnut. Escape was finally aided by a low flying ostrich, clutching a rope ladder woven from discarded purple lingerie - a little surreal, perhaps, for we all know that ostriches cannot fly and are not the most helpful of creatures.

You could easily be forgiven for waking from such a dream contemplating your sanity. Of course, there is always the distinct possibility that you are somewhat unbalanced, but don't reach for the Directory of Psychotherapists just yet.

The subconscious works in mysterious ways, emitting garbled symbolic messages, often with a surreal edge. If your mind appears to be more active by night than by day, then you'd best keep this book handy at all times - you'll discover a plethora of insightful interpretations for even the most bizarre of nocturnal encounters.

The Mad Moose Scary Dream Kit™.

Note: The editor assumes no responsibility for the random nature of this book - during production he has been tormented day and night by dreams of sushi, zeppelins and flowery flip-flops.

ANGEL

In this increasingly frantic and sometimes hostile world
we all need a little extra help sometimes. To dream of
angels can be a reminder that there is a spiritual side to
your life which can be relied upon to carry you through
even the most difficult of times.

To be in the presence of angels may also suggest that
there are situations which we cannot understand.
Some events must resolve themselves - call it fate,
or divine intervention - there are things that may
be beyond your imagination and your control and
sometimes you have to accept just that.

Divine intervention.

ANIMAL KINGDOM

CAT

A feline fantasy is usually a warning sign. Yowling, biting, scratching, black or alley cats signal deceit and slander. Only if you chase away the cat in your dream will you awake with a positive frame of mind.

DOG

Commonly considered to be a symbol of friendship, often representing how you regard your relationships with others. Barking, fighting or biting dogs don't necessarily mean trouble - just that there may be a few rocky patches to negotiate, but that you have the wherewithal to negotiate them successfully.

HORSE

A Trojan gift of a dream, so contradictory are the interpretations - sexual, financial, personal or psychological.

Generally, a lucky dream, but the details are important. To ride a horse, to feel its raw power between your thighs, is a sexual cliché; it may also indicate aspects of your life over which you are powerless or, on another level, it can mean that change is imminent.

To sense the speed and energy of a horse is symbolic of potential: horse racing is, after all, the sport of kings and you may well have the opportunity to be the sovereign in your place of work or play. Just remember, with entitlement comes responsibility.

It's important to bear in mind that a horse is difficult to control: falling off it will jolt you back to reality and force you to face your fears, intentions and purpose in life.

MONKEY

See no evil, hear no evil, speak no evil - there are enough chattering, babbling monkeys out there without you adding to the confusion.

RAT

Abandon the ship now! A dream of Titanic implications - beware rash actions and avoid taking sides in any war of words, either at work or home.

Trojan house.
(The first of many atrociously bad puns in this book.)

ALLIGATOR

Beware a friend whose smile masks hostility.

BEAR

Cuddly or grizzly, caged or free? Context determines
meaning. To dream of a cuddly bear suggests
protection, a feeling of security. A wild bear, if
threatening, may indicate the opposite - fear or
a sense of suffocation, either in life, at work or by
someone close to you.

FOX

Never forget the chickens! That cute bushy-tailed beast
up to no good, so be warned! There are some
double-dealers out there waiting for you to slip up.
Drop into a lower gear, avoid 'Slippery When Wet'
signs and you'll have nothing to fear.

LION

A king of dreams, a pointer to roaring business success
or a well-earned leap in status.

TIGER

Beware the smile on the face of a tiger - you'll find
yourself being the main course. This is a dream of bad
intentions, enmity and envy. Only if you leave the tiger
hungry will you sense relief and feel empowered
to fight another day.

ELK

It's boost that ego time for sure! You've got it made with the opposite sex. Your pulling power is running at full throttle. Get into your stride and enjoy!

GOAT

Don't do it! You are in a gambling mood but the odds are stacked against you!

Elk on John.
(Another excruciatingly painful pun, and so soon.)

CAMEL

You don't necessarily have the hump but you may be burdened by responsibilities for others. If your dream resembles a scene from Lawrence of Arabia you will triumph with flying colors - possibly in a monetary sense.

ELEPHANT

A dream you are unlikely to forget because it indicates success, wisdom and fulfillment. Even a stampede of these huge beasts - as threatening as that may seem at the time - is not a negative dream, simply a reminder that while life may well be a bowl of cherries, you have to remove the pits to enjoy the fruit.

HEDGEHOG

No prickly situations here, just an opportunity to enjoy the company of friends. Uncork the wine, get out the nibbles and relish times spent with those who really do care about you.

MOUSE

This dream screams discord, family feuds or irrationality on a scale to match the often excessive reactions to this most unlikely of household terrorists.

RABBIT

Thrift shop chic may be your style but someday you'll
be wearing Prada or Chanel. The change may well be
drastic but you will find it challenging and rewarding.
And while there may be those who envy your
good fortune you must remember that it came
through hard work.

SQUIRREL

Gathering nuts in May or in dreams offers a neon-clear
symbol: you're ignoring the rainy days to come, the snow
on the ground, the bank charges and the impulse
buying. Check back on the credit card bills and be
spare with your spending. Take note of the squirrel
and you'll stay warm and dry through the winters
that life brings.

Three virtually irrelevant elephants.

BIRDS OF A FEATHER

EAGLE

A symbol of strength and success. To dream of this bird is to be invited to celebrations, toasting your success. Should you feel threatened by an eagle you may be hampered in your journey towards achievement.

OSTRICH

A strange but happy dream of good times from completely unexpected sources. Be receptive to the bearers of unusual gifts.

OWL

Disappointment looms. Something or someone may rock you back on your heels but you must go on.

PARROT

A noisy bird and a warning - you shouldn't have to be told that gossip can rebound and that keeping your mouth shut is sometimes the only way to steer clear of trouble.

PHOENIX

To dream of this legendary bird signals rebirth - that first small step you take towards your goal will be the most important on the path to success.

VULTURE

There may be someone who doesn't have your best interests at heart but, in the long run, you will be stronger for their opposition. A vulture feeding is, surprisingly, a good omen - luck may well be on your side.

CHICKEN

Don't prepare the gravy until you've caught the bird!
Slow down for a while, give yourself time to think - even if
it's just about what's for starters.

PIGEON

All that scratching around signifies uncertainty.
If you dream of flying pigeons, the uncertainty will be
resolved in a positive way. In the meantime, don't
let the dream ruffle your feathers.

PHEASANT

Be warned of an unexpected call on your resources -
but it's nothing to panic about if you are well prepared.
If you dream of cooking and eating a pheasant, you
will have more than enough of what it takes to
arrive at your intended destination.

Pigeon contemplating the laws of pi.

DOVE

A peaceful dream, a gentle reminder of how important your personal values are to you and of why people value you.

HUMMINGBIRD

It's time to book that holiday - you deserve it. You've worked for it and the further you go the more exhilarating the experience will be.

NIGHTINGALE

You lucky dreamer! Cupid has been hard at work and guess what - he's been putting in all that overtime just for you.

PEACOCK

Too much strutting, too little thinking. Don't come on like a hurricane when a gentle spring breeze would do the job just as well, perhaps, even better.

ROBIN

Picture that tiny robin, sharp and bright in the snow - a dream of entirely positive meanings.
Follow the dream and it will be the making of you.

SWAN

To dream of a black swan can signal hard times; consider yourself warned and take precautions.
A white swan is the sign of a contented home life, supportive relationships and a quiet delight in present circumstances.

CROW

A dark dream with many interpretations. The crow is associated with death and in a dream it may also represent a decision to give up on a project or a person.

CUCKOO

You probably don't want to hear the news that's coming your way - it'll upset your plans. On the other hand, if you dream of a clockwork cuckoo you'll feel upbeat about any changes, especially if they affect your personal life.

MAGPIE

Give yourself a break. There's more than one way to overcome an obstacle and there's nothing wrong with taking the easy route for a change.

SPARROW

Busy, busy, busy! Have you been jumping from task to task, believing that activity gives meaning to your life? It doesn't. Consider why you're doing what you're doing.

The bird man of Albuquerque.

BODY PARTS

EARS

You need to listen and listen carefully! There is more to words than sound - you could be missing their real meaning.

EYES

Eyes are the windows of the soul - close them and you shut out the world. Do you just want more privacy or are you afraid of what people may see through the windows?

FACE

The look of love or the scary sight of a Halloween mask? To dream of a smiling face suggests unfamiliar pleasures, new and exciting opportunities. The opposite is true if the face is threatening.

MOUTH

Silence may be the solution to your worries and a kiss can only make your dreaming sweeter.

NOSE

Do you smell trouble? Someone may be doing a Pinocchio. Be on your guard against troublemakers and don't even think about getting into arguments that you know intuitively you cannot win.

BLOOD

Spilt blood is a sign of loss, or a fear of weakness. Nobody wants to see their life force draining away so heed the message and steer clear of trouble.

BONES

A dream traditionally representing death or fear of dying. Don't feel threatened. Just think of how great it is to be alive!

TEETH

A familiar and troubling dream. A visit to the dentist is no cause for celebration and to dream of teeth being pulled, or of losing teeth in any way, is a reminder of mortality. Fear can be a source of bravery, so there is little to be gained from worrying: live life to the full right now, every single hour of every precious day.

(Note: the caption for this illustration featured a pun so dire, the editor forbade its use.)

ARMS

Embrace the future with confidence if your dream delivers you into the strong arms of a protector. To wish to stay within the surrounds of such comfort suggests a waking life not lived to its full potential.

FEET

Tired feet? You probably wish someone, anyone, would call time-out! You need a break - both physically and emotionally. Bare feet, itchy feet, strange feet or cold feet can signify an imminent change or a challenge that will have to be faced.

HANDS

To dream of washing your hands indicates a desire for new beginnings, a wish to settle past differences and move on. Dirty, bloody or gnarled hands suggest troublesome feelings which need to be resolved.

HEART

To feel your heart beat abnormally or excessively fast may mean that real-life is telling you to listen to your body - have a medical check-up. If your heart is broken, or injured in any way, take extra care of yourself.

LEGS

To be aware of anything other than strong legs can be a warning of trying times. You may be tired of running away, tired of the treadmill of daily life. Stop running. Take the time to read a map and plan your journey - you can't run forever.

NECK/THROAT

Head held high on a strong, straight neck - a wonderful dream! You have a talent for success!

A cricked neck or sore throat is not such a good sign - let the engine idle, pull over and let the traffic pass; take your time to get back into the flow of things.
A cut throat may warn of your own ability to hurt others.

STOMACH

If the ache has disappeared when you awake, the omens are good. If you dream of flaunting navel jewelry or flexing your six-pack, don't be so arrogant as to think that others have as much interest in you as you obviously have in yourself.

Random light aircraft, two thousand feet above the Atlas Mountains, November 2002. Pilot unknown.

CANDLES

In a dream a candle can illuminate the corners of your life that need to be exposed before you can progress along its winding path. If the candle stands tall and burns with a constant flame, a turn for the better is imminent. Dying flames may signify disappointment or fear. To snuff out a candle means you know there is a part of your life that should have "The End" written after it. Don't be afraid to write it.

The designer frequently burns the candle at both ends.
Some say he's just too tight to pay the electricity bill.

CELEBRITY

Brad Pitt or Mel Gibson, Catherine Zeta Jones or Cameron Diaz - most people have a special place in their life for famous people. Just like those imaginary friends that children have, you can have a relationship with them which is entirely yours. From time to time you may drift off into that 'what if' state of mind, dreaming of your favorite star. Who wouldn't, when they're feeling under the weather, appreciate George Clooney's bedside manner, or call on Buffy's special powers when they're feeling threatened?

As long as you don't start making dates with Elvis down at the Mall, these dreams simply provide harmless moments of escapism as well as a connection to a glamorous and exciting world which, in the cold light of day, can often seem a million miles away.

CHASE

Running away from something or someone is a very common dream. Almost everyone will have experienced the fear that creeps up on you in the dead of night from being chased by a monster, a fearsome foe, a dark stranger or some nameless, faceless dread.

Sometimes the dream will have you rooted to the spot - removing the ability to run or escape to safety.
No sweat! It's simply your subconscious telling you to face up to something or someone - and you can do it.

That fear in the night should leave you stronger. All you have to do to escape is open your eyes. Keep them open, watch your back and look out for yourself - the danger will soon pass.

CLOTHING

Dreams about items of clothing are representative of how the dreamer views themself and how they wish to be viewed by others.

That perennial dream of appearing naked - stripped of the usual safe covering of clothing - has no drastic consequences. It usually means that the dreamer wishes to appear more confident or that they would like to change other people's perceptions of them.

Gratuitous nudity.

COAT

To dream of wrapping yourself in a heavy coat may mean that you are hiding something or that you fear criticism. Be more open - people you trust and regard highly will accept you for who you are.

DRESS

The meanings and interpretation of dreams change over time. In Victorian times dream-sayers would counsel women against extravagance if they dreamed of a new dress - of course most practitioners of dream analysis in that period were men! A more contemporary take on such a dream suggests that unexpected social events will provide the chance for you to enjoy yourself.
The more expensive, the more daring the item of clothing, the more likely it is that you just can't wait to get down and boogie.

GLOVES

A dream of security, both emotional and financial. Losing gloves can indicate a temporary fall-out with a friend. To find gloves suggests that there is someone out there upon whom you can really rely.

HAT

A veritable hatbox of meanings!
A new hat is a good luck dream. An old, battered hat warns of difficulties with the weekly budget. To dream of an Ascot-type hat indicates popularity, but an ill-fitting hat could signal red faces all 'round. If you happen to do a Fred Astaire, looking the part in top hat and tails, you're a dreamer that's going places. Just find yourself a partner and let the music begin.

SHIRT

To wear a clean, new shirt foretells financial success while a shabby, collar-soiled shirt suggests that your often trumpeted ambitions will be hindered by someone intent on bringing you back to reality.

SHOES

Dreaming of shoes or boots is a fortunate dream - your career, travel prospects, even love life, are in for a boost.

UNDERWEAR

Expensive, silky underwear in a dream reflects on your sexuality - it usually means that you are comfortable with who you are. If you dream of dirty or torn underwear you may harbor secret feelings of which you are ashamed. Beware the Freudian slip!

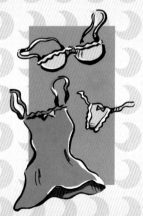

Freudian slip amongst other assorted undergarments.

COLORS

BLACK

There is menace in the Night Stalker's domain - but remember all those dark suits and 'Dynasty' shoulder pads? What were they about? Power! So, however threatening a black dream may appear, do not lose sight of the fact that it can also signify achievement.

BLUE

Dark blue sings the Blues, sad tales you'd rather leave behind. Shades of the sky above denote tranquillity and a time of calm repose among good friends.

GREEN

Green eyes, it is said, are jealous eyes - so potentially this is a dream of envy or of being envied. However, in nature, green is spring; a time of new beginnings, fresh growth and burgeoning prosperity.

PURPLE

A colorful social life may be expected, but don't let purple prose go to your head: passion without thought o principle can lead to heartache and tears.

RED

The color of fire, desire, passion and surprise. Enjoy the warmth and the excitement but shield your eyes and heart - remember Icarus whose wings were burnt by flying too close to the sun. Tread carefully and you should be fine.

WHITE

A bright, white dream shouts "Places, please!"
The curtain is about to go up! Go on, get out there.
It's your time in the spotlight. Time to perform, to bask in
the attention and to milk the applause!

YELLOW

The yellow streak of cowardice or the ribbon tied to the
bough of expectation? Your response to the shade of
yellow is important: a canary of a dream may mean that
just like Tweetie Pie you will always have the last laugh,
but a sickly shade of yellow can imply negative feelings.

*The man that dreamt of this Neptune-bound submarine
is currently undergoing extensive psychoanalysis
at an undisclosed location.*

DRINKS ALL ROUND

ALCOHOL

Dreaming of alcohol is nothing to worry about unless you find yourself falling down drunk: as in real life, being drunk in a dream suggests a tendency to lose control. If you dream of drinking in a bar your social life will be busy - surprise! surprise! - because you really know how to party when you're in the mood.

COFFEE

A great cup of coffee means fortune favors you! Drinking a bitter cup, however, suggests that you may have relationship difficulties. If you spill coffee be wary of worrying excessively about minor setbacks - they can be easily handled and will soon be forgotten.

JUICE

Relax and fear not: your needs will always be met.

MILK

Milky dreams indicate that you are in a healthy state - both in body and mind. Spill the milk or throw sour milk away in disgust and you could find yourself overstretched - be aware of your limits and you'll stay the course and sail on through.

TEA

Hot or iced, milky or black - drinking tea in a dream is a reminder that life isn't one long tea party. You can't make tea without boiling the water and won't learn any lessons unless you're prepared to take the rough with the smooth. If you're looking for rewards, perhaps it's time to put in the effort.

WATER

Drinking clear, cold water in a dream indicates stability; if you spill the water, or the water is warm or murky in any way, it is a warning. Be certain of your actions and your setbacks will have far less impact.

WINE

A generous dream, rewarding you for who you are and what you've done. However, if you over-indulge, it may be a warning message telling you to avoid running before you can walk.

If you dream of opening a choice bottle of wine with a corkscrew, then enjoy whatever comes your way - you know you're worth it!

Anonymous alcoholics.

FAILURE

A fear of failure does not recognise the boundary between being asleep and being awake. Most people endure that split second where their life hangs in the balance and everything depends upon a simple "yes" o "no" answer. The dream of failure often defines that moment but it should not be seen as wholly negative.

You may be asleep, you may be experiencing a nightmare, but you will wake up, you will make new choices, you will survive. Remember - if you hadn't already given a lot of right answers to the questions that life presents each and every day, you wouldn't be here to dream in the first place.

FAIRY

Fairies are a part of childhood experience, like Santa Claus or the Easter Bunny. To dream of a fairy may signify a need to feel protected, like a child being cozily tucked up in bed by its parents.

Similarly, your state of mind may be causing you to wish for a time when belief in the pot of gold at the end of the rainbow was entirely credible, rather than just a comforting tale.

Indulgent zeppelin picture.

FAMILY AFFAIRS

FATHER

Study the detail for the meaning. A father represents authority - in a dream he may represent protection or conflict. You may feel that life is a constant battle against a figure of authority, either within the family or at work, or perhaps you are seeking reassurance from others. Your relationship with your father in real life will color the meaning of the dream.

MOTHER

As with 'Father' interpretations, real-life relationships will shade the meaning of the dream. Generally, to dream of a mother is a positive thing, suggesting a period of stability and prosperity.

CHILD

Perceived to be a lucky omen in most circumstances, however, if you dream of yourself as a child the regression highlights your present lack of security and a wish to be protected against harsh realities.

BROTHER

For a woman, a positive dream of her brother signifies security; to be at odds with a brother may indicate resentment at being less esteemed in the eyes of a parent than her brother. For a man to dream of bonding with his brother signals security and support. A combative dream probably arises from familial conflict.

SISTER

A brother's dream of his sister signals security; for a woman the dream is less positive - jealousy or family conflict may rest at the root of the dream.

Sister Mildred - a motherly figure to numerous fathers and brothers.

FIRE

Strike a match and the potential for good or evil results.

So with dreams, certain aspects of the blaze are important to the interpretation. A building on fire can break a family's heart or bring a hefty insurance payout. If you dream of extinguishing that fire, difficult times may lie ahead, but you will find a way through them.

To be caught in a fire is not necessarily a bad thing - if you were not hurt you are probably ready to dump some excess baggage in the flames and move on, traveling lighter, faster and further.

A cheery fire in a grate means that you are contented, or seek contentment. If a fiery dream stirs strong feelings, or uneasiness, it is a warning to keep your emotions tightly under control: the strength of your feelings can save you, or, like a fire out of control, destroy everything that stands in its path.

FLOWER POWER

Just as fresh flowers brighten a room, a dream of flowers is more often than not a positive omen, suggesting happiness and caring relationships. Dead flowers caution against taking things for granted: like a garden, a relationship needs TLC to blossom and flourish.

Flowers in full bloom can also indicate a woman's delight in her own sexuality, while the budded flower is said to represent genitalia - so an element of sex and/or passion may also be present in any dream of flowers.

Unnecessary pagoda in an English country garden setting.

CARNATION

Red, white, pink or any hue - a dream of surprises.
Be responsive to others and to your surroundings and you
will be rewarded from unexpected sources.

DAFFODIL

Don't even question your current relationship - it is the
right one for you.

DAISY

True love's ways are foretold in a dream of daisies:
delight in the one you love as you would a garden
brimming with sun-kissed daisies.

DANDELION

A double-edged sword of a dream: good news if you
see them growing. Pluck them and you may find
yourself in an embarrassing situation.

FORGET-ME-NOT

You definitely won't be forgotten - you have the ability to
draw love and loyalty to you like bees to a flower.

FOXGLOVE

Friendship means much to you and you will be fortunate
in your choice of true friends.

GERANIUM

Yes, you could be the most popular person in town, but
don't be indiscriminate with your affections.
Some people may be with you just to bask in what you
have and in the long run that can drain your spirit.

HEATHER

A dream to savor, especially if the heather is white.
You will be surprised by what lies around the next corner.

HONEYSUCKLE

A dream to lift even the most weary spirit - this sweet
smelling blossom will bring bliss to lovers, creativity and
inspiration to those looking for solutions.

HYACINTH

Expect the unexpected, expect the very best!
You won't be disappointed.

Hyacinth, the office cleaner.
(Also the author of an explicit novel
featuring a variety of cleaning utensils.)

LAVENDER

The time is not for settling - be light-hearted and just enjoy yourself. Avoid making lasting promises and go easy on commitment!

LILY

Although sometimes associated with death, the lily can also represent new beginnings, rebirth and problems overcome.

ORCHID

Love and passion - sometimes out of control. Keep your head and don't be seduced by the enticing scent of these wondrously exotic flowers.

PANSY

A cautionary bloom - a dream to nudge you into doing more.

POPPY

The omens are in the opiate. Your desire for excitement and adventure may be as misleading as the smoke-filled mysteries of the opium den. Don't be fooled and don't be foolish.

PRIMROSE

A warning dream - be awake to the dangers of leaping before looking.

ROSE

Aren't you the romantic? Enjoy the beauty and the pleasure that such a dream foretells.

SUNFLOWER

If you see these often overblown flowers in a dream you may be indulging in similarly showy behavior. Be more subtle in your dealings with others - you wouldn't want the signals that you're giving out to be wrongly interpreted.

TULIP

To see these flowers in bloom suggests a period of calmness and security. Build the fire, toast the marshmallows - life can sometimes seem so sweet!

Pansy the Rottweiler.
(Addicted to beetroot and macadamia nuts.)

FLYING

The original "what am I doing with my life?" dream.

Generally, a flying dream doesn't represent dissatisfaction or anxiety - just a healthy appraisal of who you perceive yourself to be, the direction you want to take in life and how best to get there.

There may be an element of frustration in the circumstances that provoke the dream but real life is about rising above the petty restrictions that often hold us back.

Fear of flying is a different story altogether. Such a fear goes hand in hand with a sense of falling. This can indicate the dreamer's fear of failure, of living one step away from disaster. Freud would have us believe that the rush of air, the plummeting feeling, has sexual connotations. Only the individual dreamer can comment on such a dream - some dreams are so personal that a general interpretation is misleading.

Musicians sadly lacking direction.
If you would like to conduct this motley bunch,
please call the publisher urgently.

FOOD FOR THOUGHT

Eating in a dream could simply mean you have gone to bed hungry and your body is in need of nourishment.

Alternatively, eating and sexual desire have often been linked, especially when specific foods are involved: oysters, for example. To dream of sharing a meal with another person indicates your pleasure in, or desire for, a close attachment to that person.

To cook a meal for someone can highlight your desire for control or creativity; a very positive dream predicting that you have the ability to fashion a highly successful life for yourself.

If a delicious meal is shared with others it suggests a harmonious and rewarding social and family life. To eat alone, especially if you simply pick at your food, indicates loneliness, but to gorge on food, to stuff yourself full of countless delicacies, represents a personality lacking control - a greedy nature which can never be satisfied.

Where you eat also contributes to the meaning of a dream - eating at an outrageously expensive restaurant can be a warning of difficult times ahead; a meal in a comfortable restaurant with good food and pleasant surroundings predicts business or career success. If you find yourself at Joe's Diner you can expect a steady improvement in your financial position - probably because you know the value of money and spend and save accordingly.

A veritable à la carte menu of meanings exist for specific foods - you'll find a choice selection on the following pages.

ASPARAGUS

You know best! Don't let the opinions of others deter you.
Such a dream is intended to help you stand firm.

BREAD

Freshly baked bread is lucky. Stale bread symbolizes
dissatisfaction - you feel something important is missing
from your life. Return to the bakery and seek out that
fresh loaf - you need it to make sense of things.

CAKE

The sweet taste of success - dream of eating cake
and you're a winner!

CEREAL

Whether your preference is for corn flakes, oat cakes or
barley bursts, to dream of these crops has a positive
meaning. Only if you see fields spoilt by wind or rain do
you need to beware of troublesome times ahead.

CHOCOLATE

A dream reminding you that the small pleasures in life
can be just as tasty as the earth-shaking experiences
you may wish for.

EGGS

You're no bad egg - you're one of the best adverts
around for stability and good sense. Whatever you set
your sights on will come up trumps. Broken or rotten eggs
are warning you not to be an easy touch.

FISH

Good times ahead - not from luck or outside intervention, but because the plans you made were the right ones for you.

HONEY

We may no longer have access to a land of milk and honey but this dream is as sweet as it gets.
You lucky dreamer!

ICE-CREAM

Even if it's melting down your chin, a delicious dream predicting high times and rare delights.

MEAT

Fortune favors the carnivore! A meat eating dream concerns business and career, all the lights set to 'GO!'

MUSHROOMS

Just make sure it's not the deadly kind - all edible varieties predict a steady progress to Pleasantville.

Rampant cereal killer.

OYSTERS

You sexy beast! Just be careful that romance doesn't get in the way of reality or you could be left feeling empty like an oyster shell after its contents have been devoured.

POTATO

Dig them, peel them, cook them, eat them - however you see a healthy potato, it predicts a secure future entirely in your hands.

RICE

A good news dream, especially for the romantic in you. Light the candles, pour the wine and let the music play on and on and on......

ROAST DINNER

To dream of cooking a roast meal favors security and simple pleasures. Enjoyable times with close family members could be on the cards if you were carving or serving the meal.

SALT

To dream of salt predicts a full and rewarding life. You may work hard in the short term but life will repay your efforts in the long run.

TOMATO

Fun times are coming your way - be sure to enjoy them while they last.

VEGETABLES

A dream of mixed blessings. You may feel that the final piece of the jigsaw is missing, but be patient and you will find the piece of the puzzle that will help you to make sense of things.

VINEGAR

It's happening again! There's a long line of needy friends or family depending on your support. Sometimes it can feel like you've nothing left to give, but don't underestimate your own resources and all that giving will be returned, eventually, with bells on!

Sun-dried tomato, lightly dressed.

FRUIT BOWL

Fruit is usually a lucky omen unless it happens to be rotten, in which case the dream has decidedly negative meanings. Specific fruits have different meanings.

APPLE

Succulent and sweet, the apple promises due rewards; bitter or rotten apples warn against foolish behavior.

APRICOT

Dream of an apricot and put your love life on hold. All other aspects of your life are heading for overdrive - way too fast to let love take seed and grow. Dried apricots warn of people who resent your rapid progress.

BANANA

Don't ask a Freudian to interpret a dream featuring a banana! This fruit promises small blessings that will ease but not transform your life.

CHERRY

A sign of good health and a lucky omen for those thinking of becoming parents. Rotten cherries are warning you to be cautious in matters of the heart.

COCONUT

Watch the mail, check your lottery numbers - there's a pleasant surprise on its way and it's got your name on it.

FIG

Thinking about approaching someone at work you find attractive? Well don't!

GRAPES

Think of the slow but rewarding process of making wine: your plans are also for the long haul and they're good, well thought-out plans. In time you'll be supping from the glass of plenty with much to celebrate.

MELON

If you've been feeling down, a melon in your dreams is a sure sign that things are about to improve.

ORANGE

If you're worried about your problems or anxious about your friends or loved ones, an orange may creep into your dreams. There's no quick fix - you've just got to deal with the feelings and try to resolve the situation.

RASPBERRY

A melancholy dream insofar as the raspberry symbolizes regret at the passing of good times. Enjoy the memories, don't regret the past.

STRAWBERRY

Oh Happy Day! A dream of a dream - enjoy!

Beware: dangerously fruity dream territory.

HORROR

Feelings of horror or intense fear in a dream exaggerate

the conflicts you may be experiencing in your life.

The more frightening the dream, the greater the need to

face what is bothering you in waking hours.

INVISIBLE

Invisibility can be a curse or a blessing. For children it may seem like the ultimate fantasy - to be able spy on others without being seen, but it can also represent a loss of self, a fear that in life you are invisible to others and that you just don't count.

Or, perhaps you wish to become invisible.
You may just feel like hiding away for a while - taking a rest from life's never ending demands. Sometimes it can be the best remedy for stress, but don't forget - hibernation is temporary. The first rays of the warming spring sun will make you want to re-enter your world, to see and to be seen.

Our illustrator doesn't do 'horrific' and couldn't do 'invisible', hence the picture of his eccentric neighbor on a rickety bike.

JEWEL PURPOSE

AMBER

Giving or receiving amber indicates a welcome return to normality after trying times - you may even enjoy a period of exceptional luck following such a dream.

DIAMOND

These precious stones are not necessarily forever or even a girl's best friend. A dream of diamonds may be your subconscious reminding you of reality, cautioning against unrealistic hopes. If diamonds are worn by other people in a dream and you feel no jealousy but simply enjoy their captivating gleam, you may be pleasantly surprised by future events - sooner rather than later.

GOLD

Gold may symbolize ideals and accomplishments that you cherish. To find or mine gold can be a warning against being swayed by appearances; you can't tell a book by its cover - the title may be foiled in fool's gold.

If you are dressed in gold you will be rewarded for the values you hold dear. Attempting to hide the metal may indicate a desire to keep parts of yourself hidden from others. Don't allow the gold to slip through your fingers before you have realized its true value.

OPAL

Lucky you! Despite its sometimes unhappy history the opal is a positive omen. Good fortune is on its way.

PEARL

Tears before smiles, hard times before good. To dream of pearls is to be reminded that patience is needed.

RUBY

Passion is on your mind. Go with it - reciprocation
is assured.

SAPPHIRE

Wear them in a dream with caution - it could be time to
give your voice a rest and let people judge you by your
actions. To see sapphires on display or being worn by
others will boost your status and popularity.

SILVER

An improvement in financial matters is forecast, but not
without added responsibility. Silverware, polished like a
mirror, may cause you to forget the object itself, or its
intended use. Remember the poisoned chalice? An
object of great beauty can conceal a deadly message.

Ruby slippers - expensive and uncomfortable.

JOURNEY

A dream of direction, reflection, intention and change. Journeys undertaken in the dream world are seen to represent the dreamer's passage through real life.

Significant events or phases of the dream trip can be correlated to actual events and situations in the dreamer's waking world; plans, challenges, obstacles, achievements, experiences, highs and lows. If the journey is characterized by a fork in the road or the reaching of a crossroads, it may signify the need to make an important decision.

Details of the journey are also significant to interpretation: the weather, how enjoyable the trip proved to be and which means of transport were utilized during the dreamer's travels.

A train departing its station, a plane taking off or a car engine starting can all symbolize new beginnings, the undertaking of a new project or leaving something behind with a view to moving on. Cars and trains are also seen to carry meanings of a sexual nature.

The use of a map to guide you through a dream voyage may indicate the desire to find a way forward, to locate a source of inspiration or to reach an intended goal.

People encountered during the journey may also be of considerable significance. Did somebody accompany you on the trip? Were there familiar faces, obstructive individuals or obliging passers-by, only too happy to provide directions or a helping hand?

JUNGLE

Who would be lost in a jungle? An alien landscape filled with peculiar sounds, overrun by unfamiliar and seemingly dangerous creatures.

A fearsome dream jungle could be telling you that life appears to be a tangled mess of confusion, punctuated with worries and concerns portrayed by the presence of those silent, slithering poisonous snakes or prowling, razor-toothed predators. If you progressed through the jungle without a feeling of intimidation, then the dream is pushing you towards facing your fears by drawing on your inner strength and resolve.

A pleasurable jungle experience, where every turn was an exciting new discovery, signifies that you're living life to the full - exploring all avenues and thoroughly enjoying the process of doing so.

If matters of the heart weigh heavily on your mind, a jungle dream could be warning you to avoid becoming entwined in a romantic pursuit that is only likely to end in tears - probably yours.

Small, self-contained jungle in Hampstead Heath.

KEY ISSUES

DOOR

Do you feel as if a door has been slammed in your face? Perhaps you've made great efforts to get somewhere only to find that a locked door prevents you from reaching the final destination.

Doors are barriers. But a barrier can work in more than one way - is there something that you would like to shut the door on? Perhaps it's time that a phase in your life came to an end, or maybe you have strong emotions that you're attempting to suppress and shut away.

If you find an unlocked or even an open door, you may be on the brink of success; whereas a choice of doors can symbolize a multitude of opportunities.

Opening a door to another person forecasts opportunity knocking - the unexpected is about to reveal itself and new experiences are on the horizon.

KEY

Problems, problems, problems...and you just can't seem to find the solution. Well, perhaps now you can. To dream of a key may be the subconscious shedding light on a long-standing predicament, and if you found the key, perhaps a solution that has been staring you in the face all along. If the key was supplied by a friend, their influence in solving a certain problem could be crucial. Take heed, turn the key - it's time to unlock the answers or unleash the inspiration.

Slotting a key into a keyhole can also represent feelings of a sexual nature - desire or satisfaction.

PRISON/IMPRISONMENT

Sometimes the very things that constitute the important aspects of our lives can also make us feel trapped. Work, relationships, children, family and friends all demand attention and responsibility.

If you dream of being tied down or walled-in then a break from routine or even a clean break could be in order. Were there clues as to why you felt restricted? Did the dream suggest that it's time to seek a more rewarding job or greater satisfaction in your relationship?

To dream of imprisonment will often bear reference to an individual - after all, to find yourself in prison you have to be sent there in the first place. But remember, you could easily be responsible for your own confinement.

Alleviation from the situation, such as a welcome meal or kindly gesture from a captor or guard could represent somebody in your life who is willing or able to help.

Assortment of free men.

LIFE & TIMES

BIRTH

Birth may be a matter of a moment, but it is a unique one representing a period of life without control, a time when we truly rely on the kindness of others. Vulnerability may be the key here, or simply the desire to return to that unique situation of comfort and security.

The birth of a child changes almost everything and such responsibility may be daunting, the unmapped future challenging the carefully plotted route that it disrupts. A baby's cries evoke strong emotions - why is the baby crying? What can be done to calm the baby? Like life itself, a birth can be joyful or difficult, the cause for celebration or pain. If in the beginning was birth, so, inevitably, follows the learning process of life itself.

CHILDHOOD

Dreaming of a happy childhood is fortunate and to see children playing happily together indicates personal success. If the children were arguing or fighting you may well be seeking answers to questions which have been lingering at the back of your mind for far too long.

DEATH

In life we confront death, in some form or another, every day. We must also come to terms with our failure to make all the right choices and our inability to control every aspect of our lives. Life and death are two hands locked together and a dream of death, at its most basic level, reaffirms life while reminding us of our mortality.

MARRIAGE

Don't be hasty. It's too soon to borrow something old or something blue - dreams of marriage are not always celebratory. They can represent a fear of commitment, rather than a willingness to commit.

Of course, a wedding day is a landmark in life but it is also a celebration that may mask a variety of tensions - fear of loneliness, family pressures, a father bearing a shotgun rather than gifts, a passionate, hasty Vegas climax which may rapidly go stale like wedding cake left unattended. Dream of marriage and question your motives - is it what you really want or are you simply following the crowd?

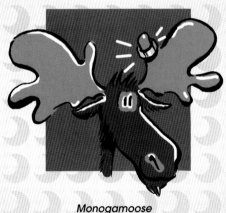

Monogamoose

LOVE & EMOTION

ADULTERY

Not surprisingly, such a dream indicates disputes with loved ones, friends and/or colleagues. It may be wise to consider your judgement when dealing with others.

To seek an affair warns of sending out the wrong signals. Resist temptation and, after a bumpy ride, you will regain control of your roller-coaster emotions.

DESERTION

A good dream if you are deserted - you have friends and loved ones to help in tough times. A bad dream if you do the leaving! Friends will be lost because you don't deserve them.

DESPAIR

A dream to sleep for! Lie back and relax - Lady Bountiful is on her way.

EMBARRASSMENT

If the blush is on you then so is a lucky star. The worse the embarrassment, the better the outcome. If others are embarrassed in your dream then trust your own instincts rather than logic to solve a problem.

FEAR

Be afraid! Be very afraid! If you wake in a cold sweat someone is going to dump on you from a great height!

JOY

A joyful dream indicates harmony, but if you watched someone else's discomfort with smirking pleasure, a past indiscretion could soon return to haunt you.

LOVE

If the loving feels good the reality will be even better, provided you think things through, take it slowly and do it right. If you watch others making whoopee and enjoy the experience, happiness is imminent, but if you are disturbed by the voyeurism, the dream is telling you to look into yourself - perhaps you are hiding something from yourself.

PARTNER

If you are at ease with your dream partner, then success is yours for the taking. Waking up with a strange partner indicates change and if that partner is of the same gender you need to think about who you are and what you really want.

As you may by now realize, this man has little sense of embarrassment.

MIRROR

Mirror, Mirror on the wall...what do you see? Do you stare in disbelief or are you happy with the reflection?

If you were frightened by your own reflection you may fear growing old, getting tired, being unable to cope. Don't be afraid - confronting mortality is something we all have to do. How you choose to do that will define your future. If your reflection in the mirror gives you pleasure beware of your own vanity - beauty is also in the eye of those who look upon you.

A broken mirror is traditionally a sign of difficult times ahead. The broken glass does not signify everlasting disaster, however, so don't be too concerned! Setbacks will only be temporary.

Voyeuristic picture of a woman in curlers.

MONEY

A dream of money shows concern about those things
you hold precious - family, career, love life or your future
plans. If you lost money in the dream it could indicate
that you're worried about the path your life
seems to be taking.

An unexpected discovery of a pot of gold, or a suitcase
full of used bank notes doesn't necessarily mean you're
destined to be rich and famous - it can be a reminder
that money isn't everything, that while you may think
your troubles would disappear with a windfall, there are
other aspects of your life which must be sorted out
before you can feel truly fulfilled.

Giving or lending money to others usually reflects on your
generous spirit although you may also be going through
a period where you feel the demands of others are
depleting your own resources.

If you hide money in a dream you may simply be
concerned about the lack of it, but if you hoard it the
dream is telling you not to be mean - loosen up,
watching interest rates is neither a particularly rewarding
nor healthy pastime.

To dream of indulging in a fabulous spending spree
suggests that any cash you spend will bring you both
pleasure and future profit.

MUSICAL MOMENTS

CELLO

Forget the Freudian stance - to string a cello and hear its sweet and low sound foretells of a good news day. A broken string, a sudden loss of melody, suggests an imminent parting from a friend.

DRUMS

Go on, admit it - you want to call the tune, you want the world to march to your beat. Just keep it simple, don't smash up the kit to impress your audience and you'll get to be Leader of the Pack - your skills and clear vision will be recognized by others.

GUITAR

Not everyone can be on the cover of Rolling Stone magazine - the dream could be revealing hidden motives. Are you playing that air guitar because you truly love the music or because you think that sex, drugs and rock 'n' roll are an easier alternative to getting up in the morning and facing the real world of work?
Time for a reality check. Every day plays a different tune - find your own and not only may you get what you need, but possibly a little of what you want, too.

TRUMPET/BUGLE

In dreams, as in life, this instrument more often than not sounds a victorious note. If the notes are jarring and discordant the opposite applies. It should be remembered that the same sound is used to signal both charge and retreat.

ORCHESTRA

If you're fortunate enough to have a dream scored for full orchestra then you're in a good place, at ease with yourself and the world around you. If the conductor loses the plot, it's time to front up to the musicians and seize the podium, even if at first you are unsure whether you are baton waving or drowning in discord.

PIANO

Major or minor, black or white keys - the piano has the capacity to either calm or arouse, chill or pacify. Expectations should be scaled down if fingers stray from the melody, but, practice does make perfect - so don't give up until the last crescendo peaks and the coda fades.

VIOLIN

Unless the dream is over-orchestrated, violins signal peace and stable relationships that can weather the occasional wrong note or broken string.

Practice makes perfect, music makes the world go 'round, sushi makes the editor nervous.

NUDITY

Maybe you're at work, with friends or strangers, in a public place, on stage, in front of cameras - suddenly... you are naked! What do you do? How do you feel? If you're embarrassed, exposure is what you fear. You may not believe in yourself, you may be afraid that you're unworthy of any attention paid to you. Learn to trust those who have given you responsibility, those who love you for who you are, warts and all.

If you're not embarrassed to be caught without a stitch of clothing to your name you have the guts and potential of the chorus girl who had to go on and save the show. You weren't born to be an understudy. You belong center stage. Get out there and milk the applause.

More gratuitous nudity.

QUARREL

Potentially a draining dream but one that offers relief
from life's many tensions. Maybe you've been spoiling for
an argument but have kept a lid on the verbals for so
long that you feel like a volcano on the
brink of eruption.

There's no need to look for trouble now.
The dream has offered a resolution, if only temporarily.
Keep calm and play it cool - confrontation is not what
you really want and harsh words rarely improve
situations. Leave the explosions in your dreams and
keep those fireworks boxed up and away from
anyone with the ability to light the fuse.

ROOM FOR IMPROVEMENT

ATTIC

You may wish to move on but there's too much still holding you in the past. Unless you sift through the debris, make a bonfire of the useless and outmoded, you will more than likely remain stuck in a rut which will increasingly limit your horizons.

BATHROOM

The bathroom is indicative of privacy and vulnerability, a room associated with fresh starts as well as finality. You may just want to wash that man right out of your hair or possibly something deeper is bothering you - it may be time to take control of your own future with clean and willing hands.

BEDROOM

Feeling safe or feeling sexy - only you know how the dream made you feel. If the bedroom is unfamiliar, a pleasant change is on the agenda.

CELLAR

If you're running scared and hiding in the cellar then heed the warning - go over any plans you may have for the future and make sure that you acknowledge both the positives and the negatives. If the cellar in your dream is welcoming rather than threatening, you can afford to ease back, take a break, enjoy life a little more.

KITCHEN

The ambience is the key to this dream: if the kitchen resembles a battlefield between armies of unwashed crockery and dirty utensils, you may be feeling down or under pressure; a warm, inviting room means that you feel safe within your circle of family and friends.

LOUNGE/LIVING ROOM

Is the scene harmonious or fretful? A comfortable gathering of family or friends indicates prosperity and well-being. An argumentative scene or a room with furnishings that resemble trailer park rejects can mean that something remains unreconciled within you. It should be faced and overcome before you can move on to a more secure and peaceful existence.

Time for pizza.

ROYAL FLUSH

KING

In spite of the fact that many kings, throughout history, have come to sticky ends, such a dream traditionally indicates a boost to your reputation.

QUEEN

We're not talking Madonna or Abba's Dancing Queen. We're talking a symbol of the past, figurehead of Church and State, of demanding deference. Maybe we all need a pat on the head from authority figures once in a while - it can't hurt the psyche to feel appreciated by someone whose wealth and position far exceeds our wildest expectations.

PRINCE

Prince of Darkness or Prince of Light?
Prince Edward or Prince the pop star?
Generally, a vivid imagination has been let loose in Dreamsville if such unlikely casting inhabits a dream. There again, the mystic casting couch may be the dreamer's only way of getting close to fame; it may be the mechanism which frees the spirit from the humdrum and paints a crimson smile on a monochromatic world.

PRINCESS

There may be only one truly iconic princess - Princess Diana, and many, many tear-stained dreams were born of her leaving. However, the age-old measures of interpretation state that to meet a princess in a dream foretells opportunities not to be missed and prestige for the taking.

Unconfirmed sighting of The King.

SEASON'S GREETINGS

SPRING

A dream to kick-start new ideas, awaken dormant
feelings. Be young in age, spirit or heart, and
never pause to doubt your dreams.

SUMMER

To dream of summer on a winter's night may reinforce
existing happiness or indicate a surprising and pleasant
turn in personal affairs. If the warmth that summer brings
delights your body, the sensation may relate to your
feelings about a partner or colleague.

FALL

Seeing drifting leaves and feeling at peace before the
winter sets in predicts domestic bliss. It can also signify
an unexpected bonus from an unlikely source
which may intensify the feelings of security
that this dream denotes.

WINTER

Darkness, cold and fearful, is impatient dreaming, waiting
for renewal and perhaps relief from
present difficulties and strife.

Vivaldi's four seasonings.

THE SKY'S THE LIMIT

MOON

To dream by the light of the silvery moon should give pleasure and usher in a period of peace and well-being.

A new moon suggests a lucky streak. A full moon is a positive force for love. A waxing moon indicates imminent change and a waning moon warns of loss.

A moon obscured by clouds has unhappy connotations unless the moon asserts its radiance and banishes the shadows from its face.

SUN

The sun in splendor warms and eases - so a dreamer may be confident, assured of what they do and who they are.

Watching the sun rise is a sign that new days and new challenges hold no fears.

A setting sun, with its sky daubed rainbow bright, suggests excitement and changes in your life that will give rise to better days.

However, a darkened, misty sun is cautionary - count the cost before committing to the act and trust your own counsel above the wagging tongues of the so-called experts.

CLOUDS

Fluffy white clouds in a bright blue sky - the omens
are good! Almost too good to be true in fact!
Aim high and you will hit your target dead center.

Gathering storm clouds can foretell difficult relationships,
but if they clear so too will any problems.

RAINBOW

Somewhere over the rainbow change is waiting.
You may not understand why life takes the turn it does
or why certain things are happening to you, but it is a
necessary process. Change is evolution - development
and growth. Embrace whatever you find at the end of
the rainbow and it will serve you well.

*Rare image of the only known
line dancing raccoon.*

COMET

This dream is of particular relevance to lovers:
it green-lights happiness with your partner and signifies
a relationship based on mutual commitment
as well as passion.

METEOR

Such a fiery object in the sky predicts rocketing success
for a brief but exciting period. Light the blue touch
paper, stand back and enjoy your moment!

PLANETS

To see distant planets in a dream doesn't mean you're
about to be abducted and enslaved to alien life-forms!
It does, however, suggest conflict between reality and
desire - you may have the soul of an intergalactic
buccaneer, yet feel trapped by daily chores and routine.
If you put your adventurous spirit to work
in the real world, it is guaranteed to pay off.
May the force be with you!

STARS

A very special dream of promise and fulfillment.
Hitch your wagon to a star and always trust its
light to guide you through.

*Since page 44 it has come to light that these musicians
have a repertoire restricted to Holst's Planet Suite.
They will be fired. (Conductor position no longer open.)*

TELEPHONE

Talk, talk, talk! Even when you're dreaming you want to be at the center of events. Is the connection good? If so, you are a pleasure to be with, always the one to offer a kind word, or tell a joke to lift the gloom.

If that careless operator has trouble connecting you, take care with your words - there may be someone looking for an opportunity to deliberately misunderstand you.

How prehistoric man survived without text messaging remains a baffling mystery.

TIME'S UP

Is it on your side or are you trying to outrun it?
A time dream can be about your desire to live outside
the confines of the clock - to escape the striking hours
which chart your journey to the future.

Perhaps that clock reminds you of how restricted you
feel; how inevitable your future seems. Sometimes you'd
like to set your imagination free and be someone else,
somewhere completely different.

Dreaming of different times of the day also reflects on
how you feel. Morning can take you back to your
childhood, or it can offer you a bright new start.

If you dream of a sky-bright noon, you will feel able
to tackle almost anything.

Afternoon suggests a winding down of something -
perhaps you've been stuck reading from the same book
for too long. There's no shame in not finishing it. Put it
back on the shelf and choose a more interesting story.

Evening can bring feelings of relief; it can be a calming
part of the day when you enjoy your own space and
take pleasure in what you have accomplished.

Night-time brings you close to those dark places you
sometimes won't admit exist. Don't be afraid of them. Just
as night and day are bound together,
so is your ability to choose between the
darkness and the light.

UMBRELLA

You need protection from more than April showers.
You want to feel safe and secure
against the driving rain.

Sometimes the wind can turn the umbrella inside out,
send it flying like tumbleweeds in a Western. If so, you
need to concentrate your efforts on building self-esteem.
You have the means to make your life secure - just
the will and your protection from the elements
will see you through even the
stormiest of weather.

*Hideous umbrella left on the
Orient Express in 1978. Never claimed.*

UNDERGROUND

Buried Alive! What a frightener!
And a relatively common dream.

The simplest interpretation suggests that you feel the
weight of the world on your shoulders - everything seems
to be closing in on you and it's difficult to know
which way to turn.

The dream can also mean that you feel
trapped between your true identity and the person
other people perceive you as. Sometimes it may feel
that life resembles an interrogation scene from a war
movie but you don't have to give up your secrets.
Always remember: nobody has the right
to invade those places in your heart
which are yours alone.

VAMPIRE

Too many late night movies? Not necessarily. You may feel drained by a situation, or by other people.

What if you were the one with the teeth and cape? A different story altogether! You'd better rethink those devious plans that you sometimes hatch - you'll need a lot more than extensive dental reconstruction for people to believe that crooked smile.

Count the draculas.

WATERY WONDER

Water constantly reacts against its boundaries whether they are formed by nature or by man: our control over it is temporary at best. And if our dream-world broodest o'er the troubled sea of the mind it is the form and the appearance of those dreams, the spectacle of life's waters, which determine meaning.

Clear water or gentle waves are fortunate omens: stormy seas or cloudy pools reflect the shadows that accompany our journey through life.

If water is the essence of life then any dream of it must, by definition, concern what is closest to our own notions of identity. Always remember - stormy weather may be frightening, but it is temporary. After showers, rainbows appear and floods are often nature's way of restoring fertility to a soil ravaged by man's greed.

Never underestimate the ability of the human spirit to survive the onslaught of nature nor your own capacity for self-preservation.

LAKE/POND/POOL

At peace by moonlight - think serenity and wholeness, but if troubled by it's wind-ripped waves, be wary of the days to follow. Reckless acts rebound with consequences which could have been foreseen.

RAIN

...just singing in the rain, what a wonderful feeling... A dream of lucky contacts, of appreciation for work done and of recognition for past favors. However, be wary of getting caught in a thunderstorm - it could be revealing a fear that your insecurities and failings may be exposed.

RIVER/STREAM

In dreams, a pleasant walk beside a flowing river indicates prosperity. If the river turns into a torrent, or if its waters darken, complacency is threatened and unpleasant change is signaled.

SEA/OCEAN

A placid sea, calm to the horizon, is a dream of well-being, but troubled waters trouble waking hours. Courage will be needed to confront a life that does not necessarily follow its predicted or intended course.

SWAMP

A troubling dream - a swamp is hardly pleasant and can signify regret and feelings of remorse which, if not addressed, could lead to long periods of self-doubt and even depression.

WATERFALL

A chance encounter may send you head over heels like a barrel over Niagara Falls - and, yes, it will undoubtedly be a pleasant fall.

Bridge over troubled waiters.

BATHING

Nakedness may indicate vulnerability, but the act of
washing indicates a willingness to shed the very things
that may shame us or hinder our progress: choose
either new beginnings or retreat to safety.

If the bath water is murky be warned that simply floating,
keeping your head above water, is never sufficient action
for realizing full potential.

DIVING

A reckless and impetuous dream.
Will you swallow dive or belly-flop? Remember to test
the water before you jump - the shallow end is not where
you want to land!

DROWNING

A dream of hopelessness: life may well feel rudderless
amidst a sea of hostile elements.

SWIMMING

Carefree skinny-dipping in clear, cool water is a lucky
dream; in muddied or rough waters help is needed
to recognise the goals you should be aiming
for in real life.

To swim in clothing indicates a fear of exposure,
but to swim with others and feel comfortable
is a sign of security.

Exceedingly dirty bath water belonging to a famous Hollywood film star whose name we dare not mention.

WINDOW

Broken windows equal broken promises or broken
dreams - perhaps new scenery is what you need.

Maybe you're looking in through the window from
outside. Feeling left out, wishing for the comfort you see?
Jump through a window and you tempt fate,
but you will also have a soft landing; your daring
will bring rewards.

To dream of opening a window means
change will bring prosperity. To close a window is to
breathe a sigh of relief, to escape something
damaging or unpleasant by
a split second.

Molar expedition: the pun ruthlessly axed from page 21.
A quick call to the printer enabled its inclusion.
(The editor will never notice, he detests reading.)

Last night I dreamt about...

Adultery	62	Cellar	70
Alcohol	32	Cello	66
Alligator	12	Cereal	46
Amber	54	Chase	26
Angel	8	Cherry	50
Animals	**10**	Chicken	17
Apple	50	Child/Children	36
Apricot	50	Childhood	60
Argument	69	Chocolate	46
Arms	22	**Clothing**	**27**
Asparagus	46	Clouds	77
Attic	70	Coat	28
Banana	50	Coconut	50
Bathing	88	Coffee	32
Bathroom	70	**Colors**	**30**
Bedroom	70	Comet	78
Bear	12	Crow	19
Birds	**16**	Cuckoo	19
Birth	60	Daffodil	40
Black	30	Daisy	40
Blood	21	Dandelion	40
Blue	30	Death	60
Body	**20**	Desertion	62
Bones	21	Despair	62
Bread	46	Diamond	54
Brother	36	Diving	88
Bugle	66	Dog	10
Cake	46	Door	58
Camel	14	Dove	18
Candle	24	Dress	28
Carnation	40	**Drinks**	**32**
Cat	10	Drowning	88
Celebrity	25	Drums	66

Last night I dreamt about...

Meat	47	Pool	86
Melon	51	Pond	86
Meteor	78	Poppy	42
Milk	32	Potato	48
Mirror	64	Primrose	42
Money	65	Prince	72
Monkey	11	Princess	72
Moon	76	Prison	59
Mother	36	Purple	30
Mouse	14	Quarrel	69
Mouth	20	Queen	72
Musical instruments 66		Rabbit	15
Mushrooms	47	Rain	86
Neck	23	Rainbow	77
Nightingale	18	Raspberry	51
Nose	20	Rat	11
Nudity	68	Red	30
Ocean	86	Rice	48
Opal	54	Roast dinner	48
Orange	51	Robin	18
Orchestra	67	**Rooms**	**70**
Orchid	42	**Royalty**	**72**
Ostrich	16	Ruby	55
Owl	16	Salt	48
Oyster	48	Sapphire	55
Pansy	42	Sea	86
Parrot	16	**Seasons**	**74**
Partner	63	Shirt	29
Peacock	18	Shoes	29
Pearl	54	Silver	55
Pheasant	17	Sister	36
Phoenix	16	**Sky**	**76**
Piano	67	Sparrow	19
Pigeon	17	Spring	74
Planets	78	Squirrel	15

...an ocean of shoes.

Unknown woman dreaming of sushi (we suspect).

Other titles in this range include:

**A SOMEWHAT OPTIMISTIC BOOK OF
SPELLS FOR EMERGENCY USE WHEN ALL CONVENTIONAL
METHODS OF CRISIS RESOLUTION HAVE FAILED**

**A SURPRISINGLY SOOTHING BOOK OF
HARMONY FOR THOSE TEETERING
ON THE BRINK OF TOTAL NEUROTIC MELTDOWN**

Sweet (and savory) dreams.